GIFFORD, Clive

Tell me about-- tennis

Published in 2009 by
Evans Publishing Ltd, 2A Portman Mansions,
Chiltern St, London WIU 6NR

© Evans Brothers Limited 2009

Editor: Nicola Edwards
Designer: D.R. Ink
All photographs by Wishlist except for page 6 © 2007 Getty Images; page 9 © Bongarts/Getty Images;
page 12 © 2007 Getty Images; page 13 © 2008 Getty Images; page 22 © 2007 Getty Images; page 23
© 2008 Getty Images; 81800297; page 26 Popperfoto/Getty Images; page 27 © Getty Images 2008/AFP

British Library Cataloguing in Publication Data

Gifford, Clive

  Tennis. - (Tell me about sport)
  1. Tennis - Juvenile literature
  I. Title
  796.3'42

ISBN-13: 9780237537241

Printed in China.

Printed on chlorine free paper from sustainably managed sources.

The author and publisher would like to thank Tom Paine, Emily Louise Robinson, Andrew Love, Gemma
Trodd, Gleanne Purcell, James Heathcote, Brian Heathcote (Coach) and the Rugby Tennis Club for their
help in making this book.

Contents

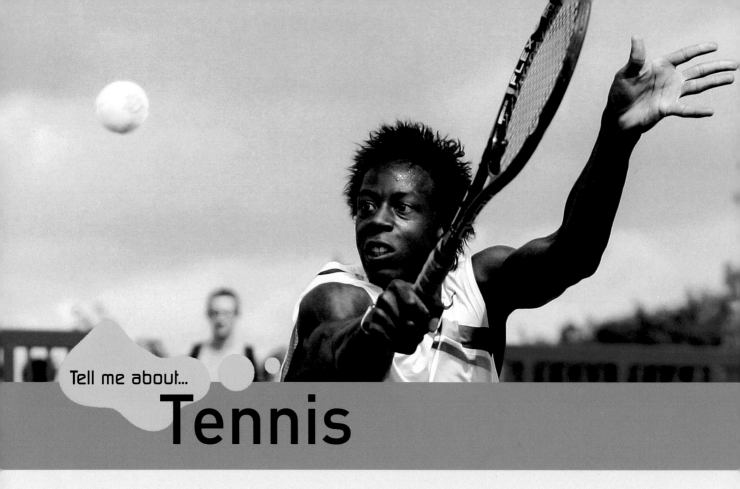

Tell me about...

Tennis

▲
French tennis star, Gael Monfils reaches for a ball during a crucial tournament match. Top players are brilliant athletes.

Tennis is an action-packed sport for two or four people. A two-player game is called a singles match. A game with four players (two per side) is called doubles. Players use a racket to hit a tennis ball around an area called a court. There are different ways of hitting the ball. These are called shots or strokes.

Tennis was once seen as a gentle pastime played by ladies in smart dresses and men in jackets. But now, it is a dramatic and exciting sport where players move with great speed and hit spectacular, powerful shots.

You can start playing tennis at any age. Young players may play a version of the game called Mini or Kanga Tennis. This is played on a smaller court

The four players move in close to the net during an exciting game of doubles. When you play doubles you need to work well with your partner. Playing both doubles and singles will help you improve as a tennis player.

with a ball that bounces high. This gives new players more time to hit the ball.

It doesn't have to cost a lot to play tennis. A junior tennis racket and tennis balls are not expensive. It is a good idea to get advice on buying the right size racket for you.

Tennis is great fun to play at or after school with your friends. Many young players decide to take things further and play in junior competitions. There, they get to push themselves to their limit and test out their shots. One day, they may even get to play at famous tournaments just like the stars.

To become a good tennis player, you must practise as often as you can. Even if you're on your own, you can practise your shots against a wall, away from a road. Tennis lessons with a proper coach are a great way to improve how you play.

Game, set and match

▼ This player has forced his opponent to send the ball up high. He can now hit a strong shot called an overhead smash. A good smash sends the ball quickly out of the opponent's reach to win a point.

In a tennis match players win points by forcing their opponent to make a mistake, or by hitting a shot into a part of the court that their opponent cannot reach.

A point starts when a player throws the ball up in the air and hits it to an opponent. This is called serving (see page18). If a player serves the ball correctly and the other player hits it back, a rally begins. The two players move around the court hitting the ball. The point continues until one player hits a winner or the other player makes a mistake.

The ball is only allowed to bounce once on your side of the court. If it bounces more than once you lose the point.

►

If you hit the ball into the net and it doesn't land on the other half of the court, you lose the point.

◄ The scoreboard shows that the players have won two games each in the third set and have one point each in the fifth game of that set. Pete Sampras (pictured) has won the first two sets.

Tennis has a unusual way of scoring. In tennis, 'love' means zero points. Look at the panel on the right. The first player to win four points (which are scored 15, 30, 40 and game) wins the game, unless the scores are tied at 40-40, or deuce. Then, one player has to win two points in a row to gain the game.

A set is made up of a number of games. The first person to win six or seven games and be two or more games ahead of his or her opponent wins the set. There is no time limit. The first player to win two or three sets usually wins the match!

Game scoring

Here is an example of how a game of tennis is scored:

Player A	Player B	Score
1 point	0 point	(15-love)
2 points	0 point	(30-love)
2 points	1 point	(30-15)
3 points	1 point	(40-15)
4 points	1 point	(Game Player A)

Marathon matches

In a 2004 men's match, Fabrice Santoro and Arnaud Clement took a record six hours and 33 minutes to finish.

At Wimbledon in 1969, Pancho Gonzalez and Charlie Pasarell played a match which went on and on for 112 games before Gonzalez won.

Rob Peterson and Ray Miller played a single rally for over nine hours in 2001. They hit an incredible 17,062 strokes!

The court and kit

Tennis is played on a rectangular court divided into two halves by a net. The edges of the court are marked with thick white lines – sidelines at the side and baselines at each end. A tennis ball is 'in' if it bounces on any part of the line. If you hit the ball and it lands outside the sideline or baseline then it is 'out' and you lose the point.

The sidelines are narrower for singles matches and wider for doubles. The space between these two sidelines is nicknamed the tramlines.

The net stands 91cm high in the middle and a little higher at the side where it is fixed to posts. Your tennis shots have to clear this net. If during play, the ball clips the net and drops onto the other side of the court, it is still in play and the point continues.

You will run around the court a lot during a game so it is vital that your trainers are really comfortable. They must fit well and offer good grip on the court. Thick sports socks help soak up sweat and stop you getting blisters.

The rest of your tennis clothing should also be comfortable and loose enough for you to move your arms and legs freely. Cotton t-shirts and shorts or a sports skirt are ideal. Many players wear sweatbands on their wrists as well.

Grass and clay

In 2007, Roger Federer and Rafael Nadal played a match on a court which had one half made of clay and the other made of grass!

Many top players have a favourite type of court. Rafael Nadal loves clay courts. He won 81 matches in a row on clay between 2005 and 2007.

▲ This player is waiting to receive the ball from her opponent. She is well dressed for tennis in a skirt, sports top and trainers.

Star players

▲ Roger Federer signs some autographs for young fans. Federer is famous for his politeness off court as well as his great skill on it.

Federer facts

By May 2008, Roger Federer had won over 39.9 million US dollars in prize money from tennis tournaments, the most by any player.

Roger has won the famous Wimbledon tournament five times in a row. The only other man to do this is Bjorn Borg.

Professional tennis players live exciting lives. Many of them become millionaires from prize money at tournaments. Some companies pay tennis stars to advertise their products, such as tennis rackets and clothing. The top professionals jet all over the world and, wherever they go, they are cheered on by thousands of fans.

Away from the noise and bustle of a major tournament, tennis players have to live a disciplined life. They eat extremely carefully and work hard on their fitness as well as practising their shots.

Almost all top players work with their coach every day. They may practise for as long as five or six hours a day on court.

The professional tennis season is very long. It starts in January and lasts until November. All the time, pro players are expected to behave well towards fans and officials even when they lose matches or are struggling to play well.

Training hard and playing dozens of matches can place great strains on a player's body. Many players suffer injuries. They then have to work really hard to regain their fitness.

▼ Spanish tennis star Rafael Nadal practises a two handed backhand shot (see pages 16-17) as his coach watches.

Forehand strokes

▲ A coach will show you a good, comfortable racket grip for forehand shots and backhand shots. You alter your grip for different shots.

Shots in tennis are divided into backhand and forehand shots. Backhand shots are where you reach across your body with the racket. You make forehand shots on the same side as your racket arm. So, if you hold your racket in your right hand, forehand shots are to your right and backhand shots to your left.

The most common forehand shot is called the forehand drive. Play this shot after the ball has bounced on your side of the court. Aim to use a smooth, relaxed swing to send the ball back low over the net.

▼ This player hits a good forehand shot with a long swing. See how her racket ends up in a high position.

Twist your waist and swing your racket back so that your front shoulder (the shoulder of the arm holding the racket) is pointing towards your target. Then, as the ball arrives, turn your waist and swing the racket forward.

Aim to hit the ball just in front and to the side of your body. The ideal height to hit the ball is between knee and just above waist height.

Players try to get in a good position nice and early so that they have time to play their shot. This is not always possible to do, so players also learn to stretch high or reach low to hit the ball at different heights.

▶
Your arm carries on swinging through after you've hit the ball. After you've played your shot, stay alert and move for your next shot.

Backhand strokes

You play backhand shots on the opposite side of the body to forehand shots. Many new players find these shots harder to get right, but they are really important to learn. Having a good backhand as well as a forehand allows you to play shots on both sides of your body.

The most common backhand stroke is the backhand drive. Watch the ball as it flies towards you and get into a good position. Aim to hit the ball between knee and waist height.

▼ This player is about to make a backhand drive. She has taken her racket back and will swing it forward to meet the ball.

▲ Here, a player makes a backhand volley. His racket meets the ball in front of his body.

Turn your shoulders to take your racket back. Then swing your arm forward from the shoulder. Keep your wrist strong and firm as you hit the ball. Your racket keeps on swinging forward after you've hit the ball.

Some players prefer to use two hands on their backhand shot. Both hands grip the racket and the player can then swing through the ball using strength from both arms. In this way players can hit the ball with a little more power.

◄

Coaching can really help improve all your shots including your backhand.

Serving and receiving

A tennis match starts when one player serves the ball and continues until the first game is won or lost. Then the other player serves a game, and so on. A serve is hit overhead but when young players are starting out, some of them may choose to serve underarm.

There are many serving rules. Both your feet have to be behind the baseline as you serve. You toss the ball up into the air and have to hit it into the service box that is diagonally opposite.

If the ball's first bounce isn't inside the correct service box, the umpire will signal a fault. Luckily, you get a second chance to serve. If this is also a fault, a double-fault is called and you lose the point.

▼ The first serve of a game is aimed into the left service box. For the next point (shown below), the server stands to the left of the middle of the court and aims the ball into the right service box.

The serve can be a good weapon. Top players hit fast and tricky serves into the corners of the service box. These are hard to return. To win a game when the other player is serving is called a break of serve.

A player receiving the ball has little time to react. He or she must judge which direction the serve will travel and what shot to play to send the ball back. If the player receiving the ball misses it completely, the server is said to have hit an ace.

Super serves

Top players can hit serves at over 200km/h. Andy Roddick holds the world record with an amazing serve of 246km/h.

Women players aren't far behind either. In 2007, Venus Williams hit a serve which reached 204km/h.

Two players have hit 51 aces in a single tennis match – Joachim Johansson and Ivo Karlovic. Both feats occurred in 2005 and despite all those aces, both players lost their matches!

▼ A serve starts with the player standing sideways to the net. The ball is thrown up high and the racket brought over to hit the ball with the arm almost stretched. The racket is angled down a little to send the ball down into the service box.

Near the net

Sometimes, you will get the chance to race towards the net. This is an attacking move. Your next shot is likely to be a volley. This means you will hit the ball before it bounces on your side of the court.

You don't need a big swing of the racket when making volleys. Instead, you hit the ball with a short, sharp punch. For this you need to keep your wrist firm as the ball and racket meet.

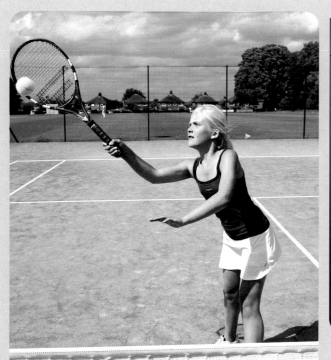

Not at the net

You must not touch the net with your racket or any part of your body or you lose the point.

The last thing you want to do is fall over the net. This happened to Rafael Nadal in practice in 2004 and he had to miss a big tournament due to injury.

Another net jumping incident that went wrong was in 1987. Ecuador's Danny Carrera tried to leap over the net after a match but tripped and broke his leg. Ouch!

 This player makes a good forehand volley. She is in the ideal position, about two paces away from the net.

You can make forehand and backhand volleys. You can also bend at the knees and get down low to play a low volley or reach up high to make a high volley. With all volleys, you must try to aim the ball away from your opponent.

If it's not you but your opponent who rushes to the net, don't panic. Try not just to hit the ball as hard as you can. Aim to hit the ball out of your opponent's reach down the sidelines.

The lob is a special stroke which you can use against a player at the net. You hit the ball high enough to pass out of their reach but so that it lands in the court behind them.

▲ The player on the right has approached the net. But his shot was easy to reach for the player on the left who has hit the ball out of his reach down the sideline.

Movement and tactics

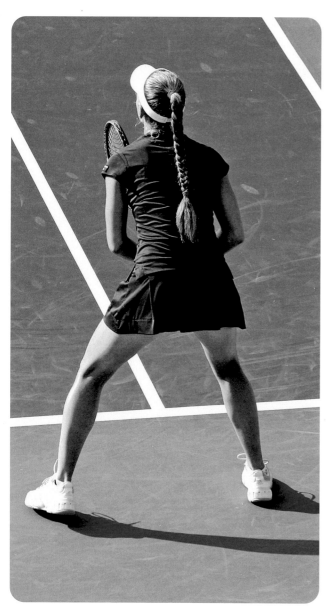

In a good ready position you should stand on the balls of your feet. Your knees should be bent a little with your feet apart. Hold your racket in front of you ready to move it to your forehand or backhand side.

Once a rally starts, you have to think hard and move fast. After playing each shot, try to move quickly to get back into a good position, ready for your next shot.

Some players like to run in towards the net after their serve and hit the ball on the volley, trying to win the point. Others prefer to stay around the baseline and play long, patient rallies, looking for an opening.

Players try to not get caught standing still, especially halfway between the net and the baseline. This area is called no man's land and it makes it easier for your opponent to beat you with a good shot.

When playing your shots, try to move your opponent around the court. A big gap might appear for you to aim your next shot at which they won't be able to reach.

When you rest between games, try to think about how the match is going. Have you spotted a weakness in how your opponent plays? Many players prefer their backhand or forehand side. Try to hit the ball where your opponent least wants it to go.

◄

Mario Ancic leaps high to hit an attempted lob by his opponent. He will aim the ball out of his opponent's reach to try to win the point.

▼ You need quick reactions to reach surprising shots by your opponent. Here, this player has sprinted and stretched to just reach the ball in time.

Tennis rules...OK!

A competitive tennis match is run by an umpire. He or she is helped by people called line judges, who watch carefully to see if the ball lands in or out. There is also a net-cord judge who signals whether a ball touches the net on a serve.

The umpire controls the game and his or her decisions are final. This official can issue warnings if players lose their temper, are rude, or break another rule such as jumping over the net or smashing a ball away into the crowd. The umpire can award points or games to the opposing player as a punishment.

Tie-breaks

If the score in a set reaches 6-6, the umpire signals a tie-break. This is a way of ending a set quickly. The first player serves for one point, then after that, each player serves for two points. This continues until one player wins the set by reaching seven or more points and having two or more points than his or her opponent.

◄

This official is called a net-cord judge. The net-cord judge checks to see whether the ball touches the net during a serve. If it does, and the serve was otherwise good, this is called a let and the player serves again.

Apart from the rules of tennis, there is something called etiquette. This is all about showing respect to your opponent and to the officials and anyone watching the game.

Etiquette includes important things such as never arguing, hitting spare tennis balls back to the server gently and only serving when your opponent is ready.

▲ In competitive matches, the tennis balls are changed regularly. Players who are about to serve with new balls hold them up to let their opponent know.

▼ Even if you're disappointed at losing, always congratulate your opponents and shake their hands at the end of the game.

If you are playing on a row of tennis courts, it also means not getting in the way of other matches. Say sorry if your ball lands on another court and wait until a point is over before going to collect it.

The world of tennis

Top tennis professionals come from all over the world. They play all over the world, too. Tournaments are held as part of tours on every continent. Some players compete at a different tournament every single week of the tennis season.

▼

In this Wimbledon doubles match, Venus Williams (right) is close to the net. Her sister, Serena, is in support behind her.

The top men's tour is called the ATP tour and the top women's tour is called the WTA tour. Players are given ranking points for winning or doing well in tournaments on the tour. These points count towards a player's world ranking. Players with a high world ranking enter the biggest tournaments without playing qualifying matches.

The four biggest tennis competitions are the Australian Open, the French Open, the US Open and Wimbledon. Winning one of these is now called winning a grand slam tournament. These four big tournaments have competitions for singles, men's doubles, women's doubles and mixed doubles. Tennis is an Olympic sport, too.

Match facts

John Pius Boland won the men's singles at the very first modern Olympics. He had turned up to be a spectator but was entered by a friend!

The last person to win all four grand slams in a year was German, Steffi Graf in 1988. She also won an Olympic gold to complete a memorable year.

The United States is the most successful country in team tennis with 17 Fed Cup wins and 32 Davis Cup wins.

Most tennis events are for individuals or for doubles pairs. The Fed Cup for women and the Davis Cup for men are team events where a series of matches are played against another country.

▼ Andy Murray plays a backhand during the 2008 US Open. The young Scot scored a notable victory over Rafael Nadal in the semi-finals only to lose to Roger Federer in the final. It was Federer's fifth US Open men's singles title.

Where next?

Here are some websites and books to help you find out more about tennis.

Websites

http://news.bbc.co.uk/sport1/hi/tennis/default.stm
Learn more about tennis at this BBC website.

http://www.wimbledon.org
Learn all about this famous Wimbledon tournament at the official website.

http://sports.espn.go.com/sports/tennis/index
This website has news about the latest tennis tournaments and the top professional players.

http://www.ontennis.com/
A huge website with everything from the rules to the legends of the sport.

http://www.lta.org.uk/Players/Juniors
The Lawn Tennis Association's website has lots of information and advice for young players.

Books

Junior Tennis by Mark Vale (Octopus and the LTA, 2002)
An in-depth book about tennis. It is full of colour photos and diagrams.

Tennis School by Naia Bray-Moffatt (DK, 2005).
A young person's guide to the skills and shots of tennis.

Tennis words

ace a serve that the opposing player is unable to reach with his or her racket and return

baseline the back line of the court which marks out the court's length

court the place where a tennis match is played

deuce when the score is 40-40 in a game

double-fault a mistake when a server fails with two serves in a row and loses the point

grand slam tournament one of the four big tournaments – Wimbledon, the US Open, the French Open and the Australian Open

grip the way that you hold your tennis racket

let a point that is replayed

lob a high shot played over an opponent and into the court behind

rally a number of shots made by players hitting the ball to each other

serve the overhead shot used to start a point in tennis

tie-break a system used in many tennis matches to end a set after the scores are tied at six games each

umpire the person who takes charge of a tennis match

volley a shot by which you hit the ball before it bounces on your side of the court

Index

Numbers in **bold** refer to pictures.